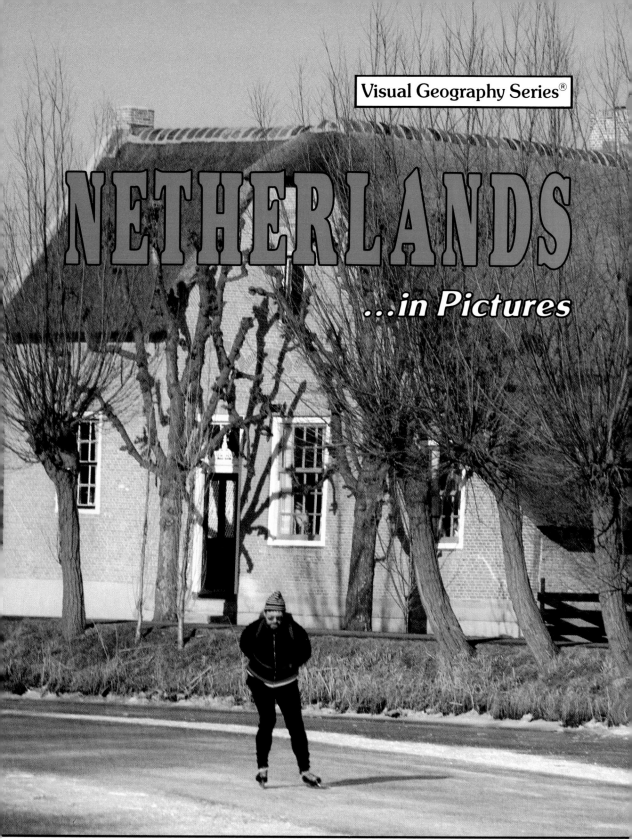

Visual Geography Series®

NETHERLANDS

...in Pictures

Prepared by
Geography Department

Lerner Publications Company
Minneapolis

Courtesy of Royal Netherlands Embassy

Dutch shoppers stroll down an arcade in Rotterdam, the major port of the Netherlands.

This book is an all-new edition in the Visual Geography Series. Previous editions were published by Sterling Publishing Company, New York City. The text, set in 10/12 Century Textbook, is fully revised and updated, and new photographs, maps, charts, and captions have been added.

LIBRARY OF CONGRESS CATALOGING-IN-PUBLICATION DATA

Netherlands in pictures / prepared by Geography Department, Lerner Publications Company.
   p. cm. — (Visual geography series)
   Rev. ed. of: Holland in pictures / Lincoln A. Boehm.
Includes index.
   Summary: Photographs and text introduce the land, history, government, people, industry, and economy of the world's most densely populated country, that has claimed ten percent of her land from the sea.
   ISBN 0-8225-1893-7 (lib. bdg.)
   1. Netherlands. [1. Netherlands.] I. Boehm, Lincoln A. Holland in pictures. II. Lerner Publications Company, Geography Dept. III. Series: Visual geography series (Minneapolis, Minn.)
DJ24.N44   1991
949.2—dc20   91–10466
                                         CIP
                                          AC

International Standard Book Number: 0-8225-1893-7
Library of Congress Catalog Card Number: 91–10466

VISUAL GEOGRAPHY SERIES®

Publisher
Harry Jonas Lerner
Associate Publisher
Nancy M. Campbell
Senior Editor
Mary M. Rodgers
Editors
Gretchen Bratvold
Tom Streissguth
Photo Researcher
Kerstin Coyle
Editorial/Photo Assistants
Marybeth Campbell
Colleen Sexton
Consultants/Contributors
Herman van der Wusten
Phyllis Schuster
Sandra K. Davis
Designer
Jim Simondet
Cartographer
Carol F. Barrett
Indexers
Kristine S. Schubert
Sylvia Timian
Production Manager
Gary J. Hansen

Independent Picture Service

Tidy farms straddle a road built on land that Dutch engineers diked and drained in the 1950s.

Acknowledgments

Title page photo by Drs. A. A. M. van der Heyden, Naarden, the Netherlands.

Elevation contours adapted from *The Times Atlas of the World*, seventh comprehensive edition (New York: Times Books, 1985).

1 2 3 4 5 6 7 8 9 10 00 99 98 97 96 95 94 93 92 91

Acres of blossoming tulips are the result of skillful planting and watering. Cut blooms and flowering bulbs (partly sprouted buds that are ready to plant) are among the main exports of the Netherlands.

Contents

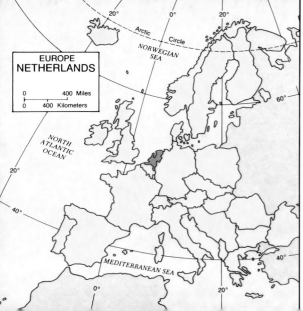

METRIC CONVERSION CHART
To Find Approximate Equivalents

WHEN YOU KNOW:	MULTIPLY BY:	TO FIND:
AREA		
acres	0.41	hectares
square miles	2.59	square kilometers
CAPACITY		
gallons	3.79	liters
LENGTH		
feet	30.48	centimeters
yards	0.91	meters
miles	1.61	kilometers
MASS (weight)		
pounds	0.45	kilograms
tons	0.91	metric tons
VOLUME		
cubic yards	0.77	cubic meters
TEMPERATURE		
degrees Fahrenheit	0.56 (*after* subtracting 32)	degrees Celsius

Built in the 1920s and 1930s, this 19-mile enclosing dam on the former Zuider Zee reaches northeastward from the province of North Holland to the province of Friesland. The barrier is not only designed to keep out the North Sea. It also offers berths for docking ships and provides a modern highway between the two provinces.

Courtesy of Royal Netherlands Embassy

Introduction

The Kingdom of the Netherlands, the most densely populated nation in Europe, is the home of 15 million Dutch. People sometimes call the country Holland, the name of a province that was long the wealthiest part of the Netherlands. The modern kingdom consists of 12 provinces, 2 of which are North Holland and South Holland.

Situated along the North Sea, much of the Netherlands lies at or below sea level.

Severe floods have occasionally brought widespread destruction. For hundreds of years, the Dutch have positioned walls and other barriers along their western coast to hold back the sea. On the protected land, the people have built farms, cities, and major ports.

Because of its location, the Netherlands became an early trading center for European goods. Over the centuries, the prosperity of the nation made it a valuable prize for stronger European powers. For example, the Netherlands came under Spanish control in the 1500s.

During the late 1600s, after the country won its independence from Spain, trade expanded and brought even greater wealth to the Netherlands. Rich Dutch merchants supported many outstanding artists, and Dutch culture flourished. The Dutch once again experienced foreign rule in 1810, when the French emperor Napoleon Bonaparte annexed the Netherlands. Four years later, French occupation ended. In 1848, under a new constitution, the Kingdom of the Netherlands established an elected parliament and made the Dutch monarch's role largely symbolic.

The new Dutch government supported private efforts to expand the nation's industries in the late 1800s. Industrial growth increased the number of urban workers. Backed by their churches, which were politically active, these laborers gradually won a broad range of social benefits, including free education and health care.

In the twentieth century, the Netherlands rebuilt industries destroyed during World War II (1939–1945) and continued efforts to protect land from the sea. In 1957 the country helped to found the European Community (EC), an economic association of European nations that follows common trade and investment policies. In the early 1990s, the advantages of EC membership were becoming more evident, as the group prepared to unite into a single market and to remove all commercial barriers. These changes are likely

Courtesy of Rijksmuseum, Amsterdam

During the 1600s, the Netherlands enjoyed a period of prosperity. Wealthy Dutch traders became patrons of art, commissioning many works. Among the era's greatest painters was Jan Vermeer, who experimented with the effects of light on his subjects. Here, in Vermeer's painting *The Milkmaid,* sunshine from a nearby window gently bathes a woman as she pours milk from a jug.

Workers build up a dike by pumping sand into a gully.

to increase Dutch trade and to stimulate the country's economy.

The history of the Netherlands involves a centuries-old struggle against the sea. But the nation's future is directed inland toward its European neighbors, with whom the Netherlands hopes to improve commercial relations.

Modern tankers and other cargo vessels pass under the Ewijk Bridge on the Waal River, which feeds into the North Sea through several estuaries (channels where rivers meet the sea).

About 1,000 windmills dot the Dutch countryside. Polder mills, which vary in size and style, are commonly seen in the western Netherlands. The job of these wind-powered mills is to pump out surplus underground water that threatens to flood the polders (drained and protected pieces of ground). The windmills empty the water into nearby canals that lead to the North Sea. In this way, the low-lying land remains dry and farmable.

1) The Land

The Netherlands is a small, flat country located in the coastal lowlands of western Europe. On the west and north, the nation is bordered by the North Sea, which is an arm of the Atlantic Ocean. Germany sits east of the Netherlands, and Belgium lies to the south. The Kingdom of the Netherlands includes the Caribbean islands of the Netherlands Antilles and Aruba. Covering an area of 16,464 square miles, the Netherlands—including its Caribbean islands —is about half the size of the state of Maine.

The word *netherlands* means "lowlands," and 50 percent of the country lies below the level of the sea. Centuries ago, early settlers built earthen walls, called dikes, and strengthened sand dunes to hold back the North Sea. With these barriers in place, the Dutch drained the water from the land to create farmland and a solid foundation for new towns.

Topography

Although the Netherlands is generally flat, geographers divide the country into two parts. The High Netherlands covers the inland provinces of Limburg, North Brabant, Gelderland, Overijssel, and Drenthe. The Low Netherlands includes the coastal provinces of Zeeland, South Holland, Utrecht, North Holland, Friesland, Groningen, and Flevoland.

HIGH NETHERLANDS

The High Netherlands occupies the eastern and southeastern parts of the country, where sandy plains and low hills mark the landscape. Within this region lies the nation's highest point, Vaalser Mountain. At 1,053 feet above sea level, the peak is 200 feet shorter than the Empire State Building in New York City.

The sandy soil of the High Netherlands supports most of the country's pine forests. Fertilizers are needed to make farming possible. In some parts of the region, the Dutch government has created nature preserves and recreational areas along ridges formed by local rivers.

LOW NETHERLANDS

Located in the western and northern parts of the country, the Low Netherlands is where the Dutch have fought their

At one time, this small piece of ground *(left)* in the province of Overijssel was surrounded by water. Efforts to reclaim land have put the island in the middle of a large, intensely cultivated field *(below)*.

Independent Picture Service

battle against the sea. To create new land in the region, the Dutch have built polders —soggy areas that are surrounded by dikes and then drained. About 5,000 polders exist, varying in size from small farming plots to the huge polders that make up the province of Flevoland. Many of the country's largest cities—including the capital of Amsterdam—sit on polders.

The clay soil in parts of the Low Netherlands is ideal for growing crops, and productive farms are common in the region. Also present are large areas of peat—partly decayed vegetation that has become packed down in layers. The peat bogs are often used as pasture for dairy cattle.

In past centuries, the Dutch dug up and dried the peat to burn as fuel. Some of

Independent Picture Service

An iron bridge crosses the Nieuwe Maas River near Rotterdam in the west central Netherlands.

these bogs then filled with water and are now inland lakes. The Loosdrecht Lakes, for example, are former peat bogs that lie between the large cities of Utrecht and Amsterdam.

Lakes and Rivers

Lakes and rivers cover about 10 percent of the Netherlands. Many centuries ago, the unchecked flow of ocean water submerged land in the northern Netherlands and formed an inland body of water called the Zuider Zee. It was divided into two parts in 1932, when Dutch engineers completed a 19-mile dam between North Holland and Friesland. This barrier formed the shallow Wadden Zee between the West Frisian (or Wadden) Islands and the mainland. The dam also entirely blocked off the remainder of the Zuider Zee, creating freshwater Lake Ijssel.

The major rivers of the Netherlands begin east and south of the country and flow westward into the North Sea. All are important to the commerce of western Europe. The Rhine River, the busy water route from Germany to the North Sea, enters the Netherlands east of the city of Nijmegen.

Smaller rivers, including the Waal and the Lower Rhine, branch off from the Rhine. The Waal flows through the Delta region—a zone of islands and peninsulas in the south central Netherlands. Another major river, the Maas, winds northward along the southeastern border of Belgium and then turns westward to run roughly parallel to the Waal.

As the Lower Rhine travels westward in the Netherlands, it changes its name twice, becoming the Lek and then the Nieuwe Maas. At the port of Rotterdam, the river enters the North Sea. A branch of the

11

Lower Rhine—the Ijssel—empties into Lake Ijssel.

Although the Schelde River lies mostly in Belgium, its broad estuary, where the river meets the sea, is mainly in the Netherlands. The Schelde's major shipping channel—the West Schelde—carries oceangoing vessels between the Delta region and the Belgian port of Antwerp.

Flora and Fauna

Planted stands of evergreen trees occupy about 7 percent of the Netherlands and account for 70 percent of the country's wooded areas. Deciduous (leaf-shedding) trees include oak, birch, beech, hornbeam, and cherry. Ashes, alders, elms, and willows thrive in areas that receive heavy rain. Various types of vegetation—ranging from heathers (evergreen shrubs) in the north to roses, linden, and buckthorn in the south—grow in the western Netherlands.

Tulips, which are often associated with the Dutch, did not originate in the Netherlands but were imported from the Middle East. Nevertheless, the flower flourishes in the country's moist, spongy soil, and Dutch gardeners have bred many new varieties over the centuries. In spring, tulips, crocuses, daffodils, hyacinths, and other colorful flowering plants blanket fields between the cities of Haarlem and Leiden.

The High Netherlands is home to most of the country's wildlife. Foxes, pine martens, and tree frogs live in the nation's southern and eastern areas. Southern Limburg supports some unusual fauna, including the dormouse, the midwife toad, and the wall lizard.

Red deer are a protected species in the forests and heathlands of Hoge Veluwe National Park, which lies near the city of Arnhem in Gelderland. A nature reserve near Amsterdam safeguards rare bird species, including the purple heron and many other marsh and water birds. Spoonbills breed on Texel Island, the largest of the West Frisian Islands.

Photo © Piotrek Gorski

Canals, called *grachten* in Dutch, crisscross Amsterdam, the capital of the Netherlands. The waterways allow small craft to transport people throughout the city.

Courtesy of Netherlands Board of Tourism

Sunshine peeks through a forest in Gelderland, a province in the eastern Netherlands.

Tulips grow profusely in the western Netherlands, especially between the cities of Leiden and Haarlem. The flower started a popular craze, called "tulipomania," in the seventeenth century, when wealthy Dutch people invested their money in tulip bulbs. Cultivation of tulips is still important to the Dutch economy, with growers able to supply about 2,000 different types of bulbs.

Photo by Drs. A. A. M. van der Heyden, Naarden, the Netherlands

Hoge Veluwe National Park shelters a small number of boars, which feed on roots, grains, and small animals. Strong and ferocious, wild boars were long hunted by European nobles and monarchs. Few boars remain in the wild on the continent.

Photo by Drs. A. A. M. van der Heyden, Naarden, the Netherlands

Storms have lashed the coasts of the Netherlands for hundreds of years, forcing the Dutch to invent new ways to push back the sea. Here, workers form the foundation of a dike by sinking a heavy, flexible mattress of twigs on which stones and earth will be piled.

In winter, if the weather is cold enough, the canals near polders freeze. Dutch athletes take advantage of the solid waterways to do some long-distance ice-skating.

Climate

The climate in the low-lying Netherlands is generally mild and wet. Winds blow mainly from the west and southwest and meet few uplands. Although weather conditions are fairly uniform throughout the country, the northern provinces tend to be a little cooler than other parts of the nation.

Many winter days in the Netherlands are overcast and damp. Amsterdam's average temperature in January, the coldest month, is 41° F. Summers bring comfortable temperatures, as well as occasional rains and cold winds from the North Sea. The capital's average temperature in July, the warmest month, is 69° F. Annual rainfall throughout the country ranges between 22 and 32 inches. The wettest areas lie near the coast and in the southern province of Limburg.

Winter mists and fogs are common, especially in the northern and western Netherlands. Coastal areas get the full force of storms from the North Sea. These powerful tempests can break through the dikes, unleashing massive floods that endanger residents and damage property. The most recent deluge, in 1953, killed 1,850 people and destroyed 48,000 homes.

To prevent such damage from happening again, the Dutch built many dams and movable storm barriers. These structures protect the land along all the river mouths on the Delta except the West Schelde, where the sea-lane to Belgium remains open.

Natural Resources

The Netherlands has limited mineral resources. Coal deposits in Limburg were first mined in the late 1800s, when demand for energy increased. After scientists found large natural gas reserves in 1959, the government closed the nation's coal mines.

The natural gas field in Groningen, near the village of Slochteren, is one of the largest in the world. Natural gas also exists in the Wadden Zee and in the North Sea. After workers dug wells in the 1960s in the Groningen Field, most Dutch homes and industries converted to natural gas, which the Netherlands also began to export. Believing that the demand for natural gas would decrease within a few decades, the Dutch government did not encourage conservation. As a result, supplies are dwindling.

The Dutch extract some petroleum in the southwestern province of Drenthe and from the floor of the North Sea, but quantities are insufficient for the country's needs. The nation's most abundant surface mineral is limestone. Formerly used as a building stone, it is now more common as a component of cement and fertilizer. River valleys provide clay for bricks and roofing tiles.

Lights glow from the equipment at an oil facility in Rotterdam, the site of Europe's largest refinery. Although some crude oil comes from Dutch platforms in the North Sea, most is imported and then made into petroleum.

Canals intersected by bridges lace the crowded, winding streets of Amsterdam. Built on a polder, the city center is not suited to modern urban traffic. As a result, many firms have moved to the edge of the capital, particularly near Schiphol Airport. This change has allowed central Amsterdam to preserve its historic character.

Cities

Most Dutch live in the west central Netherlands, a region of fertile land and many broad rivers. Nearly 90 percent of the people reside in urban areas, the largest of which are Amsterdam, Rotterdam, The Hague, and Utrecht. By law, Amsterdam is the capital, but the government meets in The Hague.

AMSTERDAM

The country's largest city, Amsterdam has nearly one million residents in its metropolitan area. Housing has long been in short supply, forcing many people to live in suburbs and in planned communities outside the city limits. Most of Amsterdam's businesses involve trade, banking, and tourism. The area near Amsterdam's Schiphol Airport is a center for many of these economic activities. Factories in and around the capital produce electrical equipment, aircraft, and processed food.

Amsterdam was named for a dam that the Dutch built on the Amstel River in the 1200s, when the city was a small fishing village. In 1482 the coastal town was walled in to protect its growing industries and trade from attacks and floods. During the sixteenth and seventeenth centuries, Am-

The Keizersgracht flows near the house of Anne Frank, a Jewish girl whose famous diary gives an account of hiding from the Germans in Amsterdam during World War II (1939–1945).

Photo © Jerg Kroener

sterdam welcomed many religious refugees. They brought new skills to the city from other parts of Europe.

The North Sea Canal links Amsterdam's harbor to the North Sea, allowing ocean-going vessels to enter the port. Within the city itself, shorter canals also provide access to the docks. More than 1,000 bridges cross the canals, which are lined with old houses that wealthy merchants built in earlier centuries.

Photo © Jerg Kroener

Patrons enjoy a warm September afternoon at a cafe on the Spiegelgracht.

Photo © Piotrek Gorski

The friendly pigeons of Dam Square in the heart of the capital draw large crowds throughout the day.

17

SECONDARY CITIES

Located on the Nieuwe Maas River, Rotterdam (population 558,800) is one of the busiest ports in the world. Its huge dock facilities, called Europort, handle cargo to and from the Netherlands, Germany, France, and Switzerland. A canal dug in the nineteenth century enables ships to travel downriver from these countries to Europort and the North Sea.

Crippled by German bombing raids in World War II, Rotterdam was rebuilt in the 1950s. The city's center now has shops and pedestrian malls designed by urban planners. Oil refineries, shipyards, and banking facilities add to Rotterdam's status as a major European trading center.

Northwest of Rotterdam is The Hague, a coastal city with a population of 449,300. Officially known as 's Gravenhage (meaning "the count's hedge"), The Hague was once the property of the counts of Holland. In the early 1900s, the city was the site of global peace conferences and eventually became the permanent home of the International Court of Justice. The Hague also hosts the Dutch parliament and the many offices that help to run the government. The city's modern economy depends on its position as a hub of national and international meetings and institutions. The nearby resort of Scheveningen also brings in income and provides jobs.

A major railway and highway junction, Utrecht lies on a branch of the Lower Rhine River. The city's 230,000 residents live amid historic houses, ancient religious buildings, and picturesque bridges. Utrecht's factories produce computer software, as well as more traditional goods like cloth, musical instruments, beer, and carpets.

Courtesy of Royal Netherlands Embassy

Flattened by bombing in the 1940s, central Rotterdam now exhibits modern architecture that incorporates new angles, clever use of natural light, and solar power.

An aerial view of The Hague shows the pointed towers of Knights' Hall, where the Dutch legislature meets.

A pleasure boat glides along a canal in Utrecht, which has become a religious hub both for Dutch Catholics and for Dutch Protestants. Beyond the canal, the 365-foot belfry of the city's Protestant cathedral dominates the skyline.

As long as 5,000 years ago, prehistoric peoples built this *hunebed,* or burial tomb, in the eastern Netherlands.

2) History and Government

Prehistoric Celtic and Germanic peoples lived in the area of the Netherlands as early as 3000 B.C. Giant graves in the province of Drenthe contain artifacts belonging to those first inhabitants. Farther north, in the modern provinces of Friesland and Groningen, later settlers built terps, or mounds, as places of safety from floodwaters.

By about 50 B.C., leaders of southern Europe's expanding Roman Empire had made contact with a Celtic people called the Belgae. They lived south of the Rhine, Maas, and Waal rivers (now the southern Netherlands and northern Belgium). Germanic groups, namely the Batavi and the Frisians, dwelt in the lowlands of the northern Netherlands.

By 15 B.C., the Romans had conquered the lands of the Belgae, adding this new territory to the Roman province of Gaul (modern France). The invaders did not completely overcome the Batavi. Instead, Rome treated them as allies who could supply soldiers for Roman armies. In the first century A.D., the Romans helped the Batavi to establish trade and large-scale farms. The Romans failed to push north of the Rhine into the lands of the Frisians, who remained largely independent.

The Franks

In the fourth century A.D., floods forced the Romans to abandon their northern outposts in what is now the Netherlands. In the early fifth century, the Germanic Franks moved westward into areas vacated by the Romans. Although they were successful in most of their conquests, the Franks could not overcome the fierce and stubborn Frisians, who continued to follow their own laws and religious practices.

By the end of the seventh century, the Franks controlled most of what is now the Netherlands except for the Frisian lands. The Franks, who followed the Christian religion, spread Christianity in the Netherlands. The faith took hold mainly through the missionary work of Willibrord in the late 600s and of Boniface, whom the non-Christian Frisians killed in 754.

In defiance of Frankish power, the Frisians controlled much of the seacoast until the eighth century. They built earthen walls around the ancient terps to protect them from the sea and used windmills to pump water out of the encircled land.

These Frisian efforts fostered the Dutch tradition of polder building.

By the late eighth century, the Frankish ruler Charlemagne had conquered the Frisian lands, making them part of his large kingdom. His realm had the backing of the Roman Catholic pope, who headed the Christian church at that time.

After Charlemagne's death in 814, the Frankish Empire was divided among his heirs. During the next 100 years, the Netherlands passed into the hands of several rulers. In 925 the East Frankish Kingdom (modern Germany) gained control of the Netherlands, which had come to be called Lorraine.

The Rise of Cities

During the ninth and tenth centuries, the people of Lorraine faced devastating floods and attacks by Viking raiders from northern Europe. Far removed from the center of German government, the people received little help in their struggle against these forces. Local lords, who felt only a weak

Saint Boniface, an English-born missionary, brought the Christian faith to the people of Germany and the Netherlands in the A.D. 700s. In his later life, Boniface returned to the lands of the Frisians, who were still largely non-Christian. They lived on the islands scattered off the Dutch and German coasts. Through preaching and teaching, he convinced many Frisians to be baptized. A hostile band of Frisians murdered the missionary in 754.

Photo by Bettmann Archive

loyalty to the German emperor, sponsored the building of more polders and dikes in the 1100s. These nobles also assembled crews to maintain the barriers.

German power in Lorraine was greatest in Utrecht, where the emperor had a residence. Elsewhere in the region, dukes and counts expanded their holdings, building castles near the mouths of important rivers. To be close to the protection offered by these fortresses, traders and craftspeople settled near the castles. In the thirteenth and fourteenth centuries, such communities grew in size and importance. Charters between local lords and these communities outlined laws of taxation, justice, and inheritance. These documents also set requirements for military service and for the provision of labor.

The chartered cities organized water councils to closely watch the polders, dikes, and canals in case these protective features needed repairing or strengthening. The growing settlements also began to develop local industries and to found guilds (trade associations). Trade was an essential activity, and ships carried wood, wine, metals, spices, and coal to many places inland and along the coast.

Coastal towns prospered as they built fleets of trading ships and established their own governments. Some cities, such

Photo by Mansell Collection

Crowded docks, ships waiting to unload their cargo, and the buzz of merchants' conversations characterized the cities that belonged to the Hanseatic League. This northern European trade and political organization included Dutch centers, such as Dordrecht and Amersfoort. The league set up legal and commercial policies that benefited all its members.

as Dordrecht, grew powerful by joining the Hanseatic League, a commercial federation that had originated in Germany. The league attempted to standardize trading customs and to protect merchant ships and towns from pirates. The league also tried to set forth common legal policies and to gain new trading privileges for its members.

Burgundian Rule

In the mid-1300s, after many small, internal wars, five nobles emerged as the most powerful leaders in the Netherlands. They were the count of Flanders, the duke of Brabant and Limburg, the duke of Gelder, the count of Holland, and the bishop of Utrecht. These nobles set up local governments, called estates, in which knights, merchants, clergy, and craftspeople could participate. Members of the various estates served on committees that monitored the nobles, who needed the estates' approval to raise money through taxes.

In 1419 Duke Philip of Burgundy (now part of France) became the count of Flanders. He began to expand his holdings through inheritance, purchase, political maneuvering, and war. In the northern lowlands, rich merchants welcomed Burgundian rule as a means of ensuring law and order, which would help commerce.

In the south, however, the wealthy trading towns of Brugge and Ghent (now cities in Belgium) resisted this threat to their independence. Despite revolts that occurred in the mid-1400s, Philip was determined to establish his authority throughout the lowlands. By the late 1450s, he had taken control of these chartered towns and limited their privileges.

To centralize his authority, Philip gathered representatives from his various holdings in 1465. Meeting in Brussels (now the capital of Belgium), this assembly marked the beginning of the States-General, which developed into the Dutch legislature. Philip also appointed a council to provide

Photo by Mansell Collection

The third duke of Burgundy, known as Philip the Good, successfully made alliances with the English and the French to gain territory in the Low Countries (now the Netherlands, Belgium, and Luxembourg). A patron of the arts, Philip also founded the Order of the Golden Fleece, a military organization of knights.

judicial and financial supervision over the lowlands.

Philip's son and successor, Charles the Bold, further strengthened the central government by creating a permanent army and by establishing a court to review decisions of provincial tribunals. Charles expanded his territory by taking Gelder in 1473 and by absorbing northern France in 1475. His aggressive activities angered his neighbors in Germany, France, and Switzerland. They declared war on Charles, who was killed in battle in 1477.

After Charles's defeat, France immediately seized the duchy (dukedom) of Burgundy. Amid this turmoil, representatives of several provinces in the Netherlands forced Mary, Charles's daughter and heir, to sign a charter that gave back important powers to local Dutch governments. In return, provincial leaders pledged to continue their financial support for the war against France.

The Habsburgs

Soon after her father's death, Mary married Archduke Maximilian of Habsburg. The Habsburgs ruled the Holy Roman Empire, which covered much of central Europe at that time. With the military help of the Habsburgs, Mary kept her territories in the Netherlands. After her death in 1482, Maximilian governed her lands in the name of their young son, Philip, duke of Burgundy.

Revolts took place in the late 1480s and early 1490s, as the Burgundians sought to keep control of prosperous Dutch towns and their trade. The various regions of the Netherlands resisted Burgundian rule, but Maximilian was not inclined to give up the valuable territory.

A statue of the Dutch philosopher Desiderius Erasmus stands in front of a restored church in Rotterdam. Erasmus traveled widely, teaching students and writing scholarly works at several European centers of learning. He vigorously promoted reforms within the Roman Catholic Church but did not support the popular movement, called the Protestant Reformation, that eventually resulted in the division of the Christian community.

A woodcut shows Maximilian of Habsburg after he had been crowned Holy Roman Emperor. His marriage to Mary of Burgundy brought the lowland provinces under Habsburg control. Between 1477 and 1493, Maximilian defended the Low Countries from French attacks.

Through the Habsburgs, the Burgundians had a strong ally in the Roman Catholic Church. But, in the late 1400s, the church's authority came under attack from people who believed it was becoming corrupt. Among the critics was the Dutch philosopher Desiderius Erasmus. Through his writings, Erasmus pressed for reform of immoral church practices and unwise political ties, which he felt degraded the church's Christian goals.

During these conflicts, Philip married Joan, the daughter and heir of the king of Spain, in 1496. By 1519 their son, Emperor Charles V, had inherited Spain, the Burgundian duchy (which included the Netherlands), and all the Habsburg lands. Charles expanded the Netherlands northward either by purchase or by conquest to include Friesland, Utrecht, Groningen, Drenthe, and Gelder.

Charles gave his attention to other parts of his large empire. He appointed representatives, called *stadtholders* (literally "place holders"), to administer the many provinces in what are now the Netherlands and Belgium. He treated these provinces as a semi-independent district within the Habsburg Empire. Although they had some powers, stadtholders were not members of royalty but rather executive officers. They met in Brussels, principally to discuss matters of taxation and to direct day-to-day affairs.

Reformation and Revolution

Throughout these centuries of growth and shifting loyalties, the people of the Netherlands remained Roman Catholic. Erasmus and other writers tried to point out areas where church reforms were needed. These ideas and further criticism of church policy led to the founding of the Protestant Reformation, which challenged the authority of the church.

Protestant ideas first spread to the Netherlands in the 1500s, when the Protestant thinker John Calvin began to preach a doctrine that urged hard work, simple tastes, and strict obedience to God's will. In response to Calvin's activities, Charles V encouraged the Roman Catholic Church to organize courts to find, try, and execute people suspected of heresy (opposition to Catholic teachings). As religious persecution increased, the northern provinces of the Netherlands—where Protestant ideas had taken firm root—united to express

Maximilian's grandson, Charles V, inherited all the Habsburg lands in the 1500s and was crowned Holy Roman Emperor by the pope in 1530. Religious conflicts, wars with France and Italy, and explorations in Mexico and Peru marked Charles's reign. Within the Netherlands, the emperor began the practice of using local leaders, called *stadtholders,* to run the lowland provinces.

their deep dissatisfaction with Charles's rule.

Weary of his long reign and disillusioned by the widespread opposition, Charles gave up his throne in 1555. Discontent worsened under his son and successor, Philip II, who grew up in Spain with little understanding of Dutch culture. Philip, who ruled both Spain and the Netherlands, stationed Spanish troops on Dutch territory and filled administrative posts there with Spaniards. He also taxed the Dutch to pay for Spain's wars against France.

To strengthen the Catholic church, Philip gave more land in the Netherlands to Catholic bishops. He also authorized an inquisition (a trial held by church officials) against Calvinists. Dutch nobles and commoners alike suffered imprisonment, expulsion, and execution because of their beliefs. To avoid arrest, thousands of Dutch Calvinists fled the country.

WILLIAM OF ORANGE

In response to these oppressive policies, a group of nobles headed by William, prince of Orange, ousted Philip's minister in the Netherlands in 1564. Another group of nobles pleaded with Spanish officials to stop the Inquisition, to allow religious freedom, and to assemble the States-General. One of Philip's advisers called these noble petitioners "beggars," and, as the revolutionary movement grew, its backers defiantly adopted this name.

Hurt by the government's soaring food prices, the common people supported the revolt by rioting and by destroying Roman Catholic property. In response, in 1567 Philip sent 10,000 troops under the duke of Alva to crush the rebellions. The duke established a council to suppress the rebels, and thousands were executed upon his orders.

William of Orange attempted to raise an army to defend the Netherlands from Spanish armies. But lack of money and too little support from the towns—which were full of Spanish troops—hindered his success. By 1572, however, William had gathered a group of rebels who operated from England. Known as the Sea Beggars, they

Photo by Bettmann Archive

Roman Catholic officials authorized the torture and execution of Dutch Protestants, known as Calvinists, in the mid-sixteenth century.

As a boy, William of Orange *(above)* spent a year in the household of Emperor Charles V and later was made stadtholder of Holland, Zeeland, and Utrecht by Charles's successor, Philip II. But in 1559, after Philip authorized the persecution of Protestants, William led the revolt against Habsburg rule that resulted in the independence of the Netherlands.

attacked Spanish ships and raided coastal towns. Within a short time, the Sea Beggars had captured the counties of Zeeland and Holland. Dutch cities began to openly defy Spanish authorities.

The duke of Alva fought back with land forces that inflicted great damage in other parts of the Netherlands. But the country's geography—with its hard-to-cross bogs, rivers, and lakes—made overland travel difficult. The terrain stopped the Spanish from quickly striking the Dutch. In 1573, after the Sea Beggars defeated Alva's fleet on the Zuider Zee, Philip called the duke back to Spain. As the fight continued, the Calvinists supported the Catholic Dutch armies that were fighting the Spaniards.

RELIGIOUS DIVISIONS

Although Catholics and Protestants joined forces to fight the Spaniards, religious views still divided the Dutch. Most Dutch Catholics lived in the southern provinces, and Dutch Calvinists resided mainly in the north. William persuaded members of the States-General in Brussels to set aside their religious differences and to unite to oppose Spanish rule. The representatives of the provinces signed the Pacification (Peace) of Ghent in 1576, a document that established as law the principle of religious freedom. The following year, provincial representatives signed the Union of Brussels, which politically allied the provinces.

In 1577 the provinces voted unanimously to reject the new Spanish governor—John of Austria—unless Philip agreed to withdraw all Spanish forces and to accept Dutch demands for religious freedom. Later that year, to avoid further warfare, Philip consented to these conditions.

Unity among the Dutch was short-lived, however. Southern leaders remained deeply suspicious of the Dutch Calvinists, and northern leaders strongly distrusted the southerners' ties to Spanish Catholics. Alessandro Farnese, who succeeded John as governor, urged the dissatisfied southern Catholics to withdraw from the Union of Brussels, offering them Spanish protection. As a result, three southern provinces, which later became Belgium, declared their loyalty to Catholicism and to Philip in 1579.

In the same year, seven northern provinces—Friesland, Holland, Gelderland, Groningen, Overijssel, Utrecht, and Zeeland—organized a new federation of their own. They signed the Union of Utrecht and in 1581 declared themselves the independent United Provinces of the Netherlands. Organized mainly for military purposes, this new nation had no single head of state. Zeeland and Holland, the two richest provinces of the new union, appointed William of Orange as their stadtholder. The Dutch continued to view this as a civilian post and did not consider William their monarch.

Photo by Edward S. Ross

Strips of cinnamon—which can be dried and ground into a fine powder—were among the spices that Dutch traders sought in Southeast Asia.

Independence and Trade

Spain did not accept the new union and from 1579 to 1609 battled the United Provinces on land and at sea. The Dutch continued their fight for independence even after a Catholic extremist assassinated William in 1584. William's son, Maurice, led a number of successful land campaigns, and the Dutch also won naval victories against the Spanish.

The war hurt Dutch trade, especially after Spain took over Portugal, which had long brought spices, silks, and other goods from Southeast Asia into Dutch ports. After the Spanish takeover, however, Dutch merchants had to find new suppliers of these imports. In 1602 the merchants formed the Dutch East India Company to trade directly with Asian countries. The Dutch government gave this private company the authority to make treaties

Courtesy of James Ford Bell Library, University of Minnesota

To increase their economic power in Asia, the Dutch made treaties with local rulers. Here, the leader of the island of Java (now part of Indonesia) meets with a Dutch naval officer to negotiate a trade agreement.

Enlarged in the 1200s for the count of Holland, Muiderslot—a castle east of Amsterdam—became a meeting place for Dutch poets, scientists, and other intellectuals in the seventeenth century.

with Asian rulers and approved the use of military force and slavery to promote trade. Within a few years, the Dutch had displaced the Portuguese as the leading traders in Southeast Asia.

The Dutch East India Company thrived. Dutch merchants ruthlessly pursued their commercial goals, sometimes killing people who refused to sell their goods to the company. In Southeast Asia, the Dutch pushed the Portuguese out of Ceylon (modern Sri Lanka), out of Malaya and Malacca (both now in Malaysia), and out of the Moluccas (in modern Indonesia). The Dutch West India Company, founded in 1621, acquired South American territory in the Portuguese colony of Brazil and in Dutch Guiana (present-day Suriname).

Trade, especially in the province of Holland and its main port at Amsterdam, flourished during lulls in the fight for independence. Among the most profitable items were tiles and other earthenware goods made near The Hague in the city of Delft. The blue-and-white Delft pottery

Investors in the Dutch East India Company gained great wealth from trade in Asia and were able to decorate their houses with fine paintings, ornate furniture, and marble fireplaces.

29

imitated fine Chinese porcelain and became popular throughout Europe.

In 1609 Spain and the United Provinces signed a truce, but by 1621 the war had erupted again. It became part of a larger conflict known as the Thirty Years' War (1618–1648). The Dutch—with the French as allies—struggled with limited success to absorb Flanders, an area now largely within Belgium. In 1648 the combatants signed the Peace of Westphalia to end the Thirty Years' War. Under the treaty's terms, Spain recognized the Netherlands as a free, self-ruling state and yielded the Caribbean islands of the Netherlands Antilles and Aruba to the Dutch.

The Golden Age

After the war, the Netherlands enjoyed great prosperity. Wealth flowed into the country from its expanding colonial and trade empire. In the mid-1600s, Amsterdam became the financial capital of Europe, and Leiden became a famous center of learning. Dutch culture and art, particularly painting, flourished during this golden age. The Dutch also expanded agriculture by draining more polders to create additional farmland and pasture.

Internal conflict also marked the golden age. The House of Orange, from which the stadtholders of Holland had come, followed Calvinism. Supporters of the Dutch thinker Jacobus Arminius disagreed with the Calvinists on several religious issues, and these differences led to political fights.

Another rivalry developed between the noble House of Orange and the merchants of Holland, who were known as Republicans. The Republicans feared that the Orangists would turn the Netherlands

Holding up two fingers in a gesture of commitment, Dutch leaders swear their loyalty to the Peace of Westphalia. It ended the Thirty Years' War (1618–1648), established the independence of the Netherlands, and declared a policy of religious toleration in the new nation.

After the Thirty Years' War ended, the Netherlands enjoyed a golden age of economic, scientific, and artistic success. One of the foremost Dutch scientists of the time was Antoni van Leeuwenhoek. Born in the city of Delft in 1632, Leeuwenhoek worked in a store that sold cloth. He used a magnifying glass to find flaws in the fabrics, and magnifications of other objects also caught his attention. Soon Leeuwenhoek switched his interest to the newly invented microscope. By skillfully grinding glass lenses, he made a very strong microscope, which he used to examine all kinds of living things—from bugs to the grime on his own teeth. Leeuwenhoek was the first person to observe bacteria and other microorganisms (tiny life forms). Because he carefully recorded his findings, he contributed to scientific knowledge and created a new field of study—microbiology.

The Golden Age of the Netherlands included achievements in the arts. The painter Rembrandt van Rijn lived and worked in the Jewish quarter of Amsterdam and used a local religious leader as the subject of *Portrait of a Rabbi.*

Dutch patrons of art liked to see their own lifestyles reflected in the works they commissioned. The painter Pieter de Hooch chose a courtyard for his gentle scene of seventeenth-century family life in the Netherlands.

31

Because of its prosperity, the Netherlands was the target of rival European powers. In the 1670s, the Dutch removed the dikes and other barriers in order to flood the land. In this way, they successfully prevented the advance of French armies on Dutch territory.

Photo by Bettmann Archive

into a monarchy. The Republican Johan de Witt governed Holland from 1653 to 1672 and successfully kept the Orangists from power. As the highest official in the union's richest province, de Witt was the strongest leader within the Netherlands.

To protect their wealth and trade interests, the Dutch became involved in several foreign wars. The French and the English formed an alliance in 1670 to destroy Dutch commercial power. In 1672 Dutch forces under de Witt failed to protect several towns from French attacks. In response, the dissatisfied Orangists revolted. As the French advanced, a mob murdered de Witt, and the States-General made William III, prince of Orange, stadtholder. The States-General hoped he could stop the French.

Under William's leadership, the Dutch pushed the French out of the western lowlands by opening the dikes and flooding the land. The Dutch navy defeated the English at sea. William regained lost territory before making peace with England in 1674 and with France in 1678.

In 1689 William and his wife, Mary, the heir to the English throne, became joint rulers of England. At this time, England was opposing attempts by the French king Louis XIV to expand his territory and power in Europe. As king of England and stadtholder of the Netherlands, William stood against France.

William died without an heir in 1702, and soon afterward Britain (formerly England) and the Netherlands declared war on France. The British won several notable victories, and their military dominance allowed them to get very favorable peace terms. At the postwar conferences, Dutch interests were largely ignored, since the Netherlands was too weak to back up its demands with force. Without strong political leadership, most provinces obeyed only local authorities.

From Republic to Monarchy

William's great-nephew, William IV, eventually succeeded him as stadtholder in 1740. During the rest of the eighteenth century, the Dutch economy declined. Portuguese, Swedish, and other European merchants improved their foreign trade and bought fewer goods from Dutch brokers. Amsterdam lost some of its importance as Europe's trading center. Governmental corruption drained funds meant to improve the economy. Costly wars against Prussia (now in Germany) and France in the mid-1700s and against Britain in the 1780s took the lives of many Dutch.

Courtesy of Rijksmuseum, Amsterdam

A commemorative coin dated 1686 lists the titles then held by William III as stadtholder of the Netherlands and as prince of Orange. By marrying his cousin Mary, a British princess, William strengthened his ties to the British royal family. By 1689 British leaders had offered William and Mary the crown. He ruled as king of Britain—as well as Dutch stadtholder—until his death in 1702.

Courtesy of Rijksmuseum, Amsterdam

In 1813 Willem Frederik, became the first king of the Netherlands as William I. During his reign, the Netherlands expanded to include Belgium and Luxembourg. The king's policies favored Dutch ways and angered the Belgians, who revolted in 1830. William gave up his throne in 1840, after being forced to recognize Belgium's independence.

A political group called the Patriots increasingly opposed the Orangists by forming their own army and by taking over the governments of some towns. With the help of powerful relatives, William V remained stadtholder until 1795. In that year, the Patriots and their strong ally France occupied the entire country and forced William to flee to Britain. Although under the influence of the French, the Patriots strengthened some democratic practices and reorganized the Netherlands into a centrally ruled republic.

In 1806 the French ruler Napoleon Bonaparte declared the Netherlands a kingdom and installed his brother Louis on the newly created throne. To Napoleon's surprise, Louis stood up firmly for Dutch rights, a position that led Napoleon to oust Louis in 1810. Napoleon then added the kingdom to his growing French Empire.

French rule in the Netherlands weakened the provincial merchant families, permitting the central Dutch government to claim more power. The state took over the Dutch East India Company and began to supervise education, which had long been in the hands of local authorities.

Attempts by Napoleon to conquer Europe brought the major European powers into an alliance against him. Warfare gradually spread across the continent. Defeats in 1813 forced Napoleon to withdraw French troops from the Netherlands. The Dutch then decided that the Netherlands should become a constitutional monarchy rather than return to a republican system of government. Dutch leaders invited the prince of Orange—William V's son—to become King William I. A new constitution in 1814 gave considerable authority to the monarch and created a two-house legislature.

The 1800s

The European alliance finally defeated Napoleon in 1815. At the postwar Congress of Vienna, the allies added Belgium and Luxembourg, which also had been under French control, to the Kingdom of the Netherlands. The victors hoped that the enlarged Netherlands would help to prevent the French from regaining power in Europe.

William I improved his country's economy by building new waterways and by establishing taxes that protected Dutch goods from competition. He ordered a new organization, the Netherlands Trading Company, to replace the old Dutch East and West India firms.

Although these changes benefited the kingdom, Belgians did not approve of William. They especially disliked the Calvinist king's efforts to control their Roman Catholic schools. Belgians also felt they deserved more power in the national government. Because of their dissatisfaction, Belgians revolted in August 1830 and drove Dutch troops from Brussels. Britain backed the cause of Belgian independence, and William accepted a settlement for the division of the kingdom in 1839. Belgium received part of Luxembourg. The remaining part became the Grand Duchy of Luxembourg, which recognized King William as grand duke.

In 1840 the Dutch forced William I to give up his throne after he announced plans to marry a Catholic noblewoman. His son William II ruled until 1849, and his grandson, William III, was in power until 1890. During these decades, liberal movements within the Netherlands prompted the Dutch government to revise the nation's constitution. Johan Thorbecke, leader of the Liberal party, directed the revisions during his three terms as prime minister.

The revisions reduced the monarch's powers and guaranteed freedom of the press, of assembly, and of religion. Voting rights were expanded, and the States-General received greater legislative powers. Other changes affected social standards, trade, and working conditions. For example, a canal linking the port of Rotterdam to the North Sea improved trade. Workers formed unions, and new laws made strikes legal. Thorbecke also enacted legislation that abolished slavery in Dutch colonies in Southeast Asia.

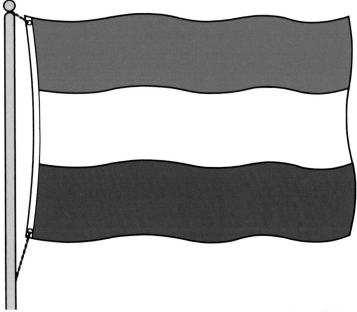

The three-part Dutch flag is based on the orange-white-blue emblem of the princes of Orange. By the late 1700s, however, the orange had been replaced by red, a change that may have been related to a Dutch desire to loosen national ties with the House of Orange.

Artwork by Laura Westlund

34

The red-brick Peace Palace in The Hague dates from the early 1900s, when Dutch leaders and other activists sought ways to establish peace in Europe. Andrew Carnegie, a wealthy U.S. industrialist, donated $1.5 million to construct the palace, and several countries gave money to furnish the interior. The Peace Palace is the seat of the International Court of Justice.

Photo by Drs. A. A. M. van der Heyden, Naarden, the Netherlands

William III died in 1890, and his successor was his 10-year-old daughter, Wilhelmina. Luxembourg's laws prevented females from inheriting the grand duchy. It thus ended its union with the Netherlands, becoming an independent state.

The World Wars

In the late 1800s, the Dutch law professor T. M. C. Asser became a spokesperson for the cause of world peace. His work led to conferences in 1899 and 1907. These meetings resulted in the establishment of the Permanent Court of Arbitration (now the International Court of Justice) at The Hague. This body provided a peaceful forum for resolving international disputes.

In line with its efforts to promote peace, the Netherlands did not take sides during World War I (1914–1918). The conflict pitted the allied nations of Britain, France, Russia, and Italy against Germany and Austria. The Netherlands's unsafe location between the warring Allies and Germans, however, made Dutch neutrality hard to maintain.

Dutch ships suffered severe damage from German submarine attacks, and the Allies took over the Dutch merchant fleet. The Dutch drafted 450,000 troops to protect the nation's borders during the conflict. After the war, the Permanent Court of Arbitration at The Hague came under the direction of the international League of Nations.

A disastrous flood in 1916 and food shortages during World War I (1914–1918) motivated Dutch engineers to build a long dam between North Holland and Friesland. The barrier would enclose part of the Zuider Zee and would offer more land for draining as farmland. Workers laid the groundwork for the barrier in 1927, beginning on the shore of each province. By 1931 only a small gap remained between the two ends of the wall *(above)*. The dam was completed in 1932 and created freshwater Lake Ijssel, as well as four fertile polders.

The social-reform movement of the late nineteenth century resumed after the war. The Dutch legislature passed laws to provide labor insurance, pension programs, and a shorter, eight-hour workday. The States-General also extended voting rights to all men in 1917 and to women in 1919. In 1929 the Netherlands and many other nations signed the Kellogg-Briand Pact, which rejected war as a means of solving international disputes.

A worldwide economic depression in the 1930s fostered the growth of restrictive regimes in many parts of Europe. In neighboring Germany, for example, Adolf Hitler and the Nazis gained power. They found support among Dutch extremists who endorsed measures to restore social and economic stability.

While the Nazis absorbed several territories on the continent, the Netherlands maintained a neutral posture. The country did, however, call up its military forces. In August 1939, Queen Wilhelmina offered her services as a negotiator in the hope of avoiding another global conflict. But Germany's invasion of Poland in September forced Britain and France to declare war.

Germany's drive to win World War II included land and air assaults on the Netherlands. On May 10, 1940, Germany invaded, leveling central Rotterdam with a swift and powerful bombardment. The Dutch army surrendered on May 14. Queen Wilhelmina and her ministers fled to Britain, where they formed a government-in-exile. The Dutch navy and merchant fleet escaped and were able to help the Allies fight the Nazis.

As the war progressed, Dutch resistance to the Nazis increased, and the occupation became more harsh. The Germans deported thousands of Dutch to work in labor camps. The Nazis sent most Dutch Jews to their deaths in extermination centers in Germany. The Germans refitted Dutch factories for their own use and seized local food supplies. In the final months of the

war, as Nazi troops retreated from the
Netherlands, they destroyed dikes, flooding vast areas. In 1945 Germany surrendered.

Postwar Recovery

After the war, substantial foreign aid
helped the Dutch to rebuild their factories,
repair their cities, and strengthen their
sea barriers. Massive flooding had ruined
Dutch farmland, but the Netherlands
avoided famine by buying food from other
countries.

During the German occupation of the Netherlands, many Dutch urban areas were bombed. Except for the bridge over
the Waal River, not much of Nijmegen—a city in the eastern part of the country—remained intact.

The dike protecting this village broke on February 1, 1953, as water from the North Sea pounded the coast of South Holland. Flooding engulfed much of the western Netherlands, ruining property and making towns into islands. Although damage in some areas was severe, the dikes held near Rotterdam, The Hague, and Amsterdam, preventing the destruction of these population centers.

Independent Picture Service

Postwar Dutch governments favored the involvement of the Netherlands in international affairs. As a result, the country became a founding member of the United Nations in 1945 and set up a trade association with Belgium and Luxembourg. In 1949 the Netherlands abandoned its traditional neutrality to participate in the North Atlantic Treaty Organization (NATO), a defensive military alliance.

Meanwhile, Dutch governments were facing difficult problems overseas. After the war ended, many Dutch colonies in Southeast Asia demanded self-rule. Fierce fighting between local peoples and Dutch troops occurred in Java, Sumatra, parts of Borneo, Sulawesi, and the Moluccas. In 1949 the Dutch government recognized the independence of these territories, which later formed the Republic of Indonesia. The Netherlands eventually gave up its other colonies in Asia and most of its South American holdings as well.

Back at home, disaster struck on February 1, 1953. On that day, the North Sea surged into the Delta region during a heavy storm and killed 1,850 people in severe flooding. Dutch engineers re-

sponded by beginning the construction of an extensive system of dams, known as the Delta Project.

In 1957 the Netherlands helped to found the Common Market (later called the European Community, or EC) to further trade and economic unity among its European member-nations. Aided by a more open European market, Dutch industrial expansion proceeded rapidly in the 1960s and 1970s. Rotterdam's new facilities for refining and storing oil made the city a major petroleum distribution center.

As a sense of economic security grew in the 1970s and 1980s, so did social concern, particularly among Dutch young people. Political activists protested the Netherlands's role in NATO, the country's housing shortage, and the nation's water pollution problem. In some cases, the protesters successfully blocked projects that threatened the environment.

Modern Challenges

The success of Dutch industry and the generous welfare system brought new challenges and problems. When oil-producing Arab states raised the price of petroleum in the 1970s, the Dutch economy declined. Dutch workers stayed away from their jobs in increasing numbers, relying instead on welfare benefits for their income. Environmental problems worsened as industries

A vast expanse of modern glass greenhouses stretches to the horizon in the western Netherlands. In these buildings, large amounts of food are grown in computer-controlled environments to provide much of the world's fresh vegetables throughout the year.

The failure of the dikes in 1953 prompted the Dutch to create the Delta Project. Begun after the flood but not completed until the mid-1980s, the plan involved partly closing off the Delta region. Storm barriers—such as this one, which defends the East Schelde—can be opened to normal tidal flow. In times of severe weather or very high tides, the barrier is closed to safeguard the nearby land.

released harmful wastes into the water, air, and soil.

In 1982 the leader of the Christian Democratic Alliance, Ruud Lubbers, began a long term as prime minister after promising to improve the economy. His cabinet operated with the support of the Liberal party. Lubbers cut spending on some welfare programs, halted plans to build or repair roads, railways, and canals, and stopped expansions of schools and hospitals.

Despite curbing some government services, Lubbers's actions were supported by most Dutch. The conservative policies have slowed rising prices, lowered the increase of the public debt, stimulated businesses, and created new jobs. The government's cutbacks, however, did not affect the completion of the Delta Project, which Queen Beatrix, the nation's monarch, officially opened in 1986.

During the national elections in 1989, social-welfare concerns and environmental issues dominated the campaign. Lubbers

promised to use more money from taxes to deal with pollution problems. Without a majority of seats in the States-General, the Christian Democrats formed a coalition (temporary combination) with the Labor party.

The coalition faced a new challenge in the early 1990s, when the members of the EC removed commercial barriers to form a single trading bloc. This important change exposed Dutch goods to increased competition and affected the nation's traditional trading and banking businesses.

Government

The Netherlands is a constitutional monarchy with a parliamentary system of government. This arrangement gives the monarch a symbolic role. The constitution assigns primary powers to the two-house States-General. The prime minister usually comes from the political party with the most seats in the States-General. Other ministerial jobs are divided among the nation's

Every September crowds watch as soldiers escort the Dutch monarch to Knights' Hall at the opening of parliament. Located in The Hague, the hall is part of a complex of buildings that houses the government.

other political parties according to the number of delegates they have in the legislature.

The upper house of the States-General has 75 members, who are elected by the provincial councils to six-year terms. Dutch voters select the 150 deputies of the lower house, who serve four-year terms. For a bill to become law, it must be discussed by the Council of State (an advisory body that reviews proposed legislation). The States-General must also approve the bill, which the monarch and the appropriate minister sign. Most bills are submitted by the ministers, but the lower house can also propose legislation and change bills.

The Dutch judiciary is independent, and all judges are appointed for life. There are no trials by jury. The supreme court, with 26 members, can strike down decisions of

Courtesy of Royal Netherlands Embassy

Beatrix *(above)* **became queen of the Netherlands in 1980, after her mother, Juliana, resigned the office at the age of 71. Dutch monarchs are not crowned. Rather they are inaugurated (introduced) in a public ceremony in Amsterdam.**

Courtesy of Royal Netherlands Embassy

Head of the Christian Democratic Alliance, Ruud Lubbers first served as prime minister of the Netherlands in 1982.

lower courts. The judiciary also includes courts of appeal, district courts, and sub-district courts. Since 1982 a national ombudsman (investigator) has had broad authority to look into disagreements between the government and citizens. The lower house appoints the ombudsman to a six-year term.

The Netherlands consists of 12 provinces, each of which is administered by a provincial council. All citizens over the age of 18 can elect council members. Each provincial council names an executive to handle daily administrative duties. The Netherlands Antilles and Aruba have their own cabinet ministers and appointed governors, who report to popularly elected legislatures.

A street scene in the capital shows the high population density typical of Dutch urban areas.

Photo © Piotrek Gorski

3) The People

Fifteen million people live in the Netherlands. With an average population density of 1,000 people per square mile, the country is one of Europe's most crowded nations. Many Dutch cities face housing shortages and a heavy strain on services. A recent decline in the birthrate to .4 percent may help to lower the pace of population growth and to relieve overcrowded cities. Nevertheless, with so many people in such a small area, the Dutch long ago realized the importance of careful urban planning.

Ethnic and Social Traits

The earliest known inhabitants of the Netherlands were Celtic and Germanic peoples. The Franks began moving into the area in the fifth century A.D. In the ninth century,

Vikings from Denmark intermarried with the population. The modern Dutch are a mixture of all of these ethnic groups.

The Dutch have long had a reputation for tolerance of different cultures and religions, even though Dutch citizens remain loyal to their own social group or faith. For example, during the 1500s and 1600s, Jews from many parts of Europe and French Protestants called Huguenots fled to the Netherlands to seek freedom from religious persecution. This tolerance also explains why some Dutch Christians protected Jews from Nazi abuse during World War II.

In the twentieth century, immigrants from former Dutch colonies, mainly Indonesia and Suriname (in South America), have arrived in the Netherlands. The country also has welcomed workers from Turkey, Morocco, and southern Europe.

Courtesy of Netherlands Board of Tourism

On Marken, an island in Lake Ijssel, a young Dutch girl wears the region's traditional costume, including wood-soled shoes.

Photo © Piotrek Gorski

In an open square, athletes practice self-defense techniques as travelers emerge from the main train station in Amsterdam.

43

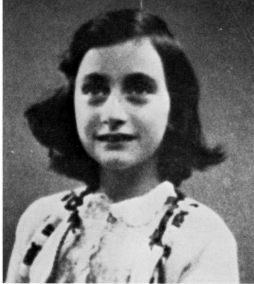

Photo by UPI/Bettmann Newsphotos

Born in 1929 in Germany, Anne Frank moved with the other members of her Jewish family to the Netherlands in 1933. They were trying to escape religious persecution by the Nazi government in their homeland. During World War II, a Dutch family allowed the Franks to hide in a secret attic in Amsterdam. While in hiding, Anne wrote down her experiences, which, after her death in a Nazi concentration camp, came to be published as *The Diary of a Young Girl*.

Photo by UPI/Bettmann Newsphotos

An estimated 50,000 squatters have occupied unused buildings in Amsterdam. Violent clashes sometimes result when the Dutch police try to reclaim the structures.

The Dutch national television network includes broadcasts in Turkish, Arabic, Italian, and other languages spoken by newcomers.

Until the 1960s, the Dutch remained closely tied to their province's or church's local culture and had little social interaction with the Dutch of different backgrounds. Since the 1960s, however, many young people have broadened their social and religious contacts. Issues that have sparked protests—including women's rights, pollution, housing, and abortion—often cut across traditional barriers.

In urban areas, shortages of housing and recreational space have caused increasing social problems in recent decades. Some homeless people, known as squatters, have taken over abandoned buildings.

Religion and Holidays

Two religious faiths have strong Dutch histories. Roman Catholicism predominates in the south, and Protestantism is common in the north. Beginning in the mid-1800s, to reduce conflict between Roman Catholics and Protestants, the Dutch established *verzuiling* (meaning "columning"). Under this system, separate religious organizations operated independent schools, clubs, political parties, newspapers, and radio stations for their members. Much of the verzuiling system has declined since the 1960s, as more Dutch have loosened their religious ties.

Traditional ways remain vital in rural areas, where families tend to be faithful to the teachings of their church. In the early 1990s, about 20 percent of the population of the Netherlands belonged to the Dutch Reformed Church, of which the monarch is usually a member. Twelve percent of the Dutch followed other Protestant faiths. About 36 percent are Roman Catholics. Roughly 30 percent of the people claim no religious affiliation.

Many Dutch holidays have religious ties. On December 5, for example, people cele-

A Dutch schoolboy gives his sister a lift home from their school in Overijssel—a province that has expanded with the creation of new polders.

Futuristic architecture characterizes the University of Technology in Delft.

brate St. Nicholas' Eve, when a person dressed as Saint Nicholas rides through the streets of Amsterdam. Bells, loud cannons, and cheering crowds greet his arrival. The Dutch exchange gifts on this day as well as on December 25.

Spring is also a time of many celebrations. On Easter, games that involve colored eggs are popular, and other sporting events take place on Easter Monday. The people mark Queen's Day on April 30 with parades, fairs, and contests. During flower festivals held in the spring, the Dutch use tulips and other plants to decorate floats.

Education

The verzuiling system originally established most Dutch schools, which have received public funding since 1917. Private school boards or local public councils are responsible for running these institutions. The country's literacy rate is 98 percent.

Children may begin attending primary school at age four, and education becomes compulsory at age five. Primary instruction lasts eight years, with English becoming part of the curriculum in the final year. Since schooling is required through age sixteen, all children advance to secondary

45

The largest Gothic cathedral in the Netherlands lies in 's Hertogenbosch, the capital of North Brabant. Parts of this Catholic church date from the 1200s.

schools, of which there are three types— general, pre-university, and vocational. Tests place pupils in the type of school that best fits their abilities and interests.

General secondary schools are classified as junior (offering a four-year course) or senior (five-year course). After six years of study, pre-university students may apply for entrance to an institution of higher education. Vocational schools offer many kinds of career preparation.

Eight universities and five technical institutes provide postsecondary education. The oldest university, at Leiden, was founded in 1575 by William of Orange. The University of Groningen was established in 1614, and the University of Utrecht opened in 1636. The Dutch government funds all institutions of higher learning, whether public or private.

Health and Welfare

The Netherlands has a complex social-welfare system. Families with children receive allowances, as do widows and orphans. The state provides health and dental insurance for all citizens who earn less than $18,000 per year. Retirement benefits are very generous. All Dutch who are unemployed for any reason receive funds that equal about three-fourths of their former wages.

In recent decades, as unemployment benefits grew more plentiful, so did the number of Dutch workers claiming to be sick or disabled. In the early 1990s, employees were absent from work about 9 percent of the time. One-fourth of Amsterdam's residents were living on welfare benefits. Growing absenteeism and tougher educational requirements for new jobs caused labor shortages and unemployment in the Dutch economy.

The Dutch benefit from an excellent system of health care. The average life expectancy of a baby born in the Netherlands in 1991 was 76 years, compared to 50 years in 1900. As in other industrialized countries of western Europe, the major causes of death in the Netherlands are heart disease, cancer, and traffic accidents.

Private organizations operate most health-care facilities in the Netherlands, and a number are still associated with churches. Medical costs are paid through the national health-insurance system. Home nursing organizations—which are also private—provide health care for the elderly, for pregnant women, and for children.

Language and Literature

The Netherlands's two official languages —Dutch and Frisian—are of Germanic origin. Frisian predates Dutch by several hundred years. Until the end of the fifteenth century, the Dutch tongue was common in northern Germany as well as in the Netherlands. About 25 dialects of Dutch are still spoken. Interest in preserving unique Dutch vocabularies and pronunciations has increased in recent years.

Some of the most noted Dutch writers discussed philosophy and law. The Dutch thinker Desiderius Erasmus, for example, was born in Rotterdam in 1467 and became a Roman Catholic priest in 1492. His philosophy, which came to be called humanism, stressed the qualities of tolerance, kindness, devotion, and honesty. Erasmus

Courtesy of Royal Netherlands Embassy

Children romp on the playground equipment in front of their housing development in Amsterdam.

Courtesy of Giraudon, The Louvre

The German painter Hans Holbein created this portrait of Desiderius Erasmus penning a letter. The Dutch thinker corresponded with many of the sixteenth century's greatest scholars.

Max Havelaar savagely criticized the behavior of the Dutch toward the local people in Dutch colonies. Published in 1860, the book caused many Dutch to demand fairer treatment of colonial peoples. As a result of this public outcry, the national legislature began to reform its colonial policy.

Most modern Dutch poets and novelists are well known only in the Netherlands and in northern Belgium, where Dutch is widely spoken. A few authors, including Harry Mulisch, have been translated. In recent years, some young Dutch writers have published their works in both English and Dutch to reach a wider readership.

Visual Arts

The rich culture of the Netherlands is particularly strong in the visual arts. In the 1400s, the works of Dirck Bouts con-

wrote during the Protestant Reformation, when Europe was torn by religious differences between Catholics and Protestants. He sought reforms that would keep the Christian community together.

Hardly known outside his native country, the Dutch poet Joost van den Vondel wrote inspiring verse about biblical subjects in the seventeenth century. In the same period, Huigh de Groot's scholarly works in Latin and Dutch about law and history found a wide audience. The parents of another philosopher of the time, Baruch Spinoza, fled to the Netherlands from Portugal, where they had been persecuted for following the Jewish faith. Spinoza grew up as a free-thinker and developed liberal religious and political ideas that were influenced by René Descartes, a French writer living in the Netherlands.

While he was a colonial administrator in Southeast Asia, Edouard Douwes Dekker wrote under the name Multatuli. His novel

Courtesy of Library of Congress

Born in Amsterdam, Baruch Spinoza ground glass lenses to make money and wrote philosophical works in his spare time. He believed strongly in the vitality of the human mind, which he felt could lead the individual to a deep understanding of the world.

Jacob van Ruisdael's painting *The Mill* shows a storm gathering along the Dutch coast in the seventeenth century. Although highly regarded now, Ruisdael's canvases did not sell well during his lifetime, and he became a doctor to support himself.

veyed unusual psychological depth. The fantastic visions of Hieronymus Bosch inspired *The Garden of Earthly Delights,* which he painted in about 1500. A few years later, the movement called the Leiden School improved the technical aspects of painting and popularized realistic forms. Worldly scenes—such as *The Chess Players* by Lucas van Leyden—gradually replaced sacred themes as subjects for Dutch painters.

An unusual feature of Dutch paintings of the golden age of the 1600s is that many portray everyday scenes. Members of the Dutch upper-middle class, who were the main patrons of art, wanted artists to create works that showed middle-class life. During this period, Rembrandt van Rijn (1606–1669) excelled at many types of painting, including portraiture. One of his most famous paintings, *The Night Watch,* depicts a militia company. Frans Hals, Rembrandt's contemporary, also achieved fame for portraiture. His richly colored canvases of everyday events convey realism and spontaneity.

The works of Jan Vermeer often include natural light coming in through latticed windows. He spent his whole life in Delft, where he painted ordinary scenes with great skill and sensitivity. Here, a geographer holds his measuring instrument while gazing outside.

49

The foremost painter of the Dutch Golden Age was Rembrandt van Rijn. Although his portraits of Amsterdam's citizens were very popular, he also painted himself, his family, landscapes, and peasant scenes. Rembrandt used light and shadow to create a somber mood, which distinguished his canvases from other paintings of the period.

Many other artists excelled during the golden age. Showing an unusual use of light, the works of Jan Vermeer (1632–1675) portray restful scenes of Dutch middle-class life. Jan Steen painted domestic settings, and the canvases of Jacob van Ruisdael capture the dramatic quality of the Dutch landscape and skies. Willem van de Velde painted magnificent seascapes, and Pieter de Hooch depicted life in the spacious homes of Dutch merchants.

The nineteenth century brought another flowering of Dutch art that reached creative heights in the works of Vincent van Gogh (1853–1890). In 1888 van Gogh moved to Arles, France, where he produced a large number of canvases. His technique, which used thick dabs of paint and intense colors, gives his artworks a strong feeling of movement.

In the twentieth century, De Stijl (meaning "the style") painters and architects helped to revolutionize the world of art and architecture. This group favored simple lines and minimal decoration. Among the most famous De Stijl artists were Piet Mondrian and Theo van Doesburg. Architects in the movement included Gerrit Rietveld, Willem Dudok, and Jacobus Johannes Pieter Oud. Modern Dutch architects have changed the appearance of urban buildings by using large glass windows to let in sunlight and by introducing brightly colored exteriors.

A carouser and gambler, Frans Hals created works that celebrate his enthusiasm for living. Although he often painted officials in their fancy uniforms, he also delighted in bringing to life images of talented musicians, laughing children, and happy couples.

Born in 1853, Vincent van Gogh failed at several professions, while continuing to paint and sketch. He created several solemn self-portraits, which depict him as sad and lonely. Van Gogh gave his works a strong emotional content and liked bright colors and thick globs of paint. Depressed about his lack of success as a painter, van Gogh killed himself at the age of 37. Critics now acknowledge him as one of the most original artists the world has ever produced.

Courtesy of Minneapolis Public Library and Information Center

Photo by Drs. A. A. M. van der Heyden, Naarden, the Netherlands

After German bombing leveled Rotterdam, Dutch architects went to work creating an entirely new city center. One designer used tilted yellow cubes on stone columns to achieve a feeling of open space in a small area. The plan also allowed the buildings to have greater exposure to sunlight.

With their arms linked behind them for balance, Dutch skaters glide past a windmill on a frozen canal. Water sports, including boating and fishing, are popular in all seasons.

Sports and Recreation

Sports are very popular in the Netherlands. The government estimates that at least four million people compete through sports clubs, and at least an equal number participate in informal recreational activities.

Among the country's largest sporting organizations is the Royal Netherlands Football (soccer) Association, which has about one million members. In the 1970s, the skills of Johan Cruyff, a top player in Europe at that time, helped the Dutch national team to emerge as an international contender. In 1988 the Dutch won the European soccer championship.

Tennis, another favorite sport, attracts about 500,000 Dutch enthusiasts. Track and field, swimming, sailing, hockey, and volleyball are also popular. The Dutch use bicycles for riding, racing, and transportation. Some areas of the country have unique traditional activities. In Friesland, for example, athletes participate in *fierljeppen*, which involves vaulting over a wide ditch with the help of a long pole.

In winter many Dutch enjoy long-distance skating on the smooth ice of the country's frozen canals. If the weather is cold enough to freeze the canals, as many as 17,000 people compete in the Elfstedentocht race. During this event, participants skate along the waterways that connect 11 towns in Friesland. In most years, temperatures have not dropped low enough for this 124-mile race to take place.

Food

Dutch cooks are known for preparing tasty, filling dishes in a simple manner. Butter is commonly used, but spices and thick sauces are not traditional features of Dutch cuisine. Immigrants from former

Dutch colonies in Southeast Asia have introduced spicier dishes in recent years.

The Dutch usually eat a small breakfast consisting of bread, rolls, thin slices of Edam or Gouda cheese, and meats such as sausage. The midday meal is also moderate, often made up of bread, cold meat slices, cheese, and a small side dish.

Dutch families gather for a large evening meal at about 6:00 P.M.—a fairly early hour by European standards. Dinner may begin with soup, followed by a dish made with vegetables and beef or bacon. Popular snacks include waffles smothered in whipped cream or in a warm caramel sauce. As a treat at any time, the Dutch enjoy chocolate that is processed locally using imported cacao beans.

A worker applies a wax coating to a brick of Dutch cheese before it can be stored and aged. Favorite national cheeses include Edam and Gouda, which are named after cities that lie in North Holland and South Holland, respectively.

Shoppers browse at an outdoor fruit market in The Hague.

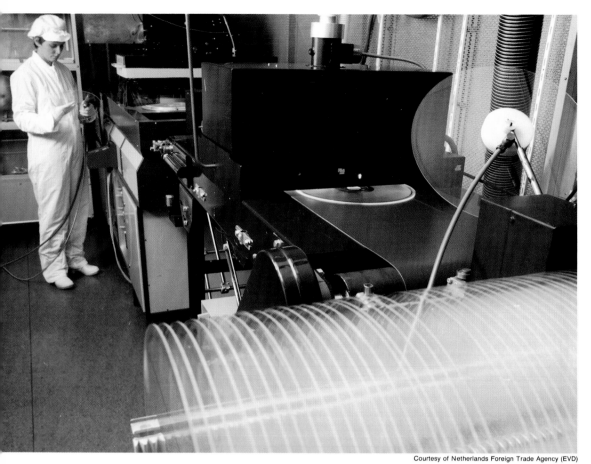

At Eindhoven in the southern Netherlands, a technician monitors the work of lasers that mold compact disks.

4) The Economy

The Dutch economy, which recovered rapidly from the destruction caused by World War II, continued to expand until 1973. In that year, economic growth slowed, partly because of a worldwide rise in oil prices. The number of jobs in Dutch industry declined. The result was a jump in unemployment, from 3 percent in 1973 to 17 percent in 1983.

After the oil crisis ended, world trade began to expand. A boom in exports in the

1980s led to financial recovery in the Netherlands. To help industry, the government cut business taxes and loosened regulations that Dutch companies found restrictive. By 1985 the unemployment rate had begun to fall.

Since the end of World War II, the Netherlands, Belgium, and Luxembourg have cooperated closely in economic matters. These small countries—together called the Benelux nations—became members of a

Skill, patience, and a steady hand are needed to shape diamonds into valuable gems. The stones easily reflect light if small angles, or facets, are cut into the sides. A talented diamond cutter knows how to make the cuts at the right size, angle, and place in the stone.

larger European organization, the Common Market. It evolved into the European Community (EC). Throughout the 1980s and in the early 1990s, the Netherlands worked within these economic associations to improve and expand its trade and investment opportunities.

Industry and Trade

The Netherlands did not develop large-scale industries until about 1890, when coal mining, chemical manufacturing, and electrical businesses were established. Since then, the country has become highly industrialized, primarily through the efforts of private companies. Foreign investment helped to finance the nation's economic growth after 1950.

The industrial sector accounts for about 70 percent of the nation's exports and employs 30 percent of the work force. The leading industrial products are chemicals, petroleum, metals, processed foods, and

The Netherlands is an innovator in many areas of manufacturing. This bus, for example, runs on energy stored in the brake system to reduce the air pollution caused by traditional exhaust pipes.

55

tobacco. Dutch companies have recently expanded their output of such high-technology products as microcomputers and precision eye equipment. Shipbuilding, an age-old Dutch industry, has declined in importance in recent years.

Trade has long been the lifeline of the Dutch economy. Germany is the Netherlands's leading trade partner, primarily because the Rhine River, a busy commercial route, links the two countries. The Dutch have also sold large supplies of natural gas to Germany. The unit of Belgium-Luxembourg ranks second to Germany as a Dutch trading partner, followed by France, Britain, and Italy.

Thirty percent of all goods shipped to or from western European countries pass through Dutch seaports. Rotterdam's Europort expanded its facilities in the 1970s and 1980s to include petrochemical, oil, and other manufacturing complexes. A deep channel dug in the North Sea allows the port to handle heavy tankers. Rotter-

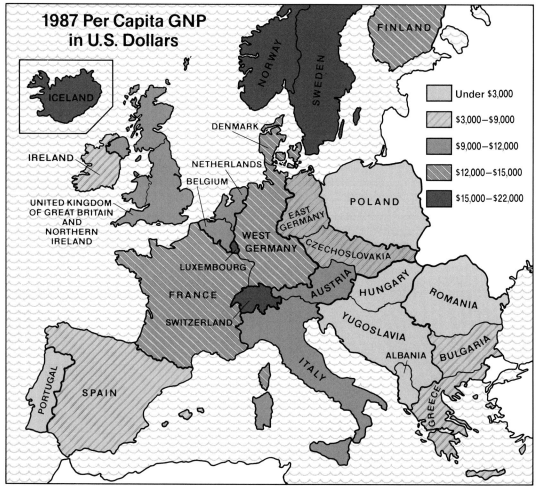

Artwork by Laura Westlund

This map compares the average productivity per person—calculated by gross national product (GNP) per capita—for 26 European countries. The GNP is the value of all goods and services produced by a nation in a year. To arrive at the GNP per capita, each country's total GNP is divided by its population. The resulting dollar amount is one measure of the standard of living in each nation. The Netherlands's figure of $11,800 reflects the country's economic recovery in the 1980s. By 1987 Dutch exports were rising, and unemployment was falling. (Data taken from *Europa World Yearbook, 1989*.)

dam is now among the world's chief oil ports and markets. Oil is bought and sold there daily, and pipelines move the petroleum from Rotterdam to Germany and Belgium.

Agriculture

Although only about 4 percent of the Dutch are engaged in farming, agriculture is still a very important part of the nation's economy. Most farms in the Netherlands are small, family-owned operations, but the government has encouraged farmers to combine their holdings into larger estates to increase agricultural efficiency.

About 65 percent of the country's land is used for agriculture, but the Netherlands still does not grow all the different foods it needs. More than 60 percent of the farmland is pasture. A further 32 percent is devoted to crop cultivation, and 6 percent supports horticulture (the growing of fruits and flowers). The Netherlands produces enough flowers and dairy products to export.

Independent Picture Service

Black-and-white holsteins graze in the province of Friesland. Dairy herds provide milk that is made into cheese, butter, milk powder, and condensed milk.

The country's five million dairy cattle are the basis of a large milk-processing industry. Breeds of Dutch dairy cattle, particularly holsteins, are known widely as high-yielding milkers. Dutch cheeses —notably Edam and Gouda—and other Dutch milk products are exported throughout the world.

Dutch farmers also raise nearly 14 million pigs and 7 million sheep. The Netherlands imports large quantities of grain to feed its livestock. Pork, mutton, and poultry are shipped to EC partners and to other parts of the world. In recent years, Dutch environmentalists have become concerned about sewage and other wastes from pigs and cattle that pollute groundwater supplies.

The most significant outdoor crops are potatoes, sugar beets, and wheat. Farmers plant corn as fodder (food for livestock). Small farms produce fresh fruits and vegetables for local consumption and for export. Farmers grow other foods in greenhouses. To make their businesses profitable, greenhouse owners have adopted energy-saving measures on a large scale.

Courtesy of Netherlands Foreign Trade Agency (EVD)

A market gardener boxes fresh heads of lettuce in a Dutch greenhouse. Nearly all of the crop is exported, and many European countries receive their shipment of lettuce on the same day that it is packed.

57

Photo by Ministry of Agriculture, Nature Management, and
Fisheries/Information and External Relations Department

Buyers sit in booths equipped with microphones as they bid on flowers at the huge Aalsmeer auction. Held every day near Amsterdam, the sale moves thousands of blooms and bulbs to world markets.

Flowers and bulbs are among the most important Dutch agricultural exports. The flower industry consists of about 8,000 small, family-owned businesses that have a long-established tradition of cooperating with each other. Individual Dutch growers often specialize in one type of plant. For instance, tulip producers do not cultivate any other type of flower. Farmers obtain seeds from specialists who work to improve plant varieties. Teams of scientists at testing stations provide vital support by sharing new knowledge with growers.

Although Dutch tulips are perhaps the most famous flowers from the Netherlands, roses are more commonly cultivated, followed by chrysanthemums, carnations, tulips, and lilies. Merchants at the Aalsmeer auction near Amsterdam sell about 12 million cut flowers and 1.5 million potted plants every day.

Transportation and Energy

The Netherlands has a varied and well-developed transportation network that links railways, roads, and water routes.

Photo by Ministry of Agriculture, Nature Management, and
Fisheries/Information and External Relations Department

A man and his sons gather armfuls of chrysanthemums from one of their greenhouses. Most flower businesses are family-owned operations.

A 19-mile road runs along the barrier dam on the Zuider Zee. The highway links North Holland and Friesland.

The country's 2,000 miles of railways run on electricity. Of the 54,400 miles of roads, roughly half are intercity highways. Several toll-free superhighways are connected to the extensive German road system.

One-third of Dutch commercial traffic moves over the country's system of inland waterways, which is longer than its rail network. The rivers of the Netherlands also carry goods from Amsterdam and Rotterdam—the country's main ports—to other parts of Europe.

Another connection to Europe and the world is through the national airline, Royal Dutch Airlines (KLM). The Netherlands's major airport, Schiphol near Amsterdam, represents a major economic asset in the nation's business connections with Europe and other continents. Smaller Dutch airfields are located near Rotterdam, Maastricht, Eindhoven, and Groningen.

Dutch ports together rank third in the world in the amount of cargo they handle, much of it involving the importing and exporting of natural gas and petroleum. Access to both these fuels has made the Netherlands a major energy producer. Small reserves of natural gas in the north

Standing for *Koninklijke Luchtvaart Maatschappij* (Royal Dutch Airlines), KLM flies to most of the world's largest cities.

Tankers and cargo vessels crowd the docks at Rotterdam, where oil and other goods stream in and out of the port every day.

As cows graze, a container ship chugs up the North Sea Canal, which connects Amsterdam to the Atlantic Ocean.

are now being worked in order to conserve the larger deposits in the huge Groningen Field. Natural gas meets about half of the country's energy needs.

Royal Dutch Shell, a multinational corporation, operates oil platforms in the North Sea. Most crude oil is imported, however, and is then refined and exported. Nuclear power supplies about 6 percent of the energy used in the Netherlands.

Fishing and Mining

Fishing is not as important to the Dutch economy as it once was. Since the 1970s, overfishing in the North Sea has caused a rapid decline in the population of herring —the principal Dutch catch for many centuries. The Netherlands's few remaining herring trawlers ply the Atlantic as far as Iceland in search of this popular fish. Fishing boats travel southward for plaice and sole, and other vessels bring in shrimp off the Dutch coast.

Perch, pike, eel, and other freshwater species once populated Lake Ijssel and the rivers of Zeeland. Pollution from the Rhine and other river systems, however, has largely wiped out supplies of those fish.

The rising cost of coal mining caused the Dutch to abandon operations in southern Limburg in the 1960s and 1970s. Natural gas in Slochteren and in the North Sea replaced coal as an energy source. The

Machinery dredges a ditch for an underground natural-gas pipeline. Although lacking most other fuels, the Netherlands has large deposits of natural gas.

Courtesy of Royal Netherlands Embassy

Independent Picture Service

Dutch fishermen help each other mend nets. Many of the country's age-old fishing villages died out when the barrier dams and storm gates were installed. The protective walls hampered access to fishing grounds in the North Sea and regulated tidal flows that brought in fish.

Dutch had changed many homes and factories to run on natural gas before realizing that stocks of the fuel were declining sharply. Although the Netherlands still exports natural gas, efforts to conserve domestic supplies are under way. In the late 1970s, oil deposits in the North Sea competed in volume with the gas finds. Dutch oil platforms now dot the surface of this stormy arm of the Atlantic Ocean.

Tourism

About five million people visit the Netherlands each year, and the nation earns more than $2 billion annually from tourism. Travelers interested in history and culture are attracted by the country's 700 museums, including the Rijksmuseum in Amsterdam, the Mauritshuis in The Hague, and the Palace of Het Loo in Apeldoorn.

Courtesy of Netherlands Board of Tourism

Scheveningen, a resort near The Hague, offers vacationers opportunities to fly kites, to suntan, and to swim.

Dutch towns and cities have distinctive characters. Amsterdam—with its canals, bridges, and seventeenth-century houses —is also a dynamic, modern city. The Hague, the official residence of Queen Beatrix, contains many parks and shopping arcades, and nearby is the seaside resort of Scheveningen. Largely rebuilt since World War II, Rotterdam is famous for its enormous port facilities and futuristic architecture.

Biking along the level roads of the Netherlands is a favorite outdoor activity for summer visitors. Most tourists arrive during the flower season from March to September. In those months, millions of tulips, daffodils, and hyacinths carpet South Holland.

The Future

In the coming decades, the Netherlands will be making some serious economic choices. Its natural gas supplies are dwindling, causing the loss of an important source of revenue. The Netherlands will have to find new energy sources, and they will likely be costly.

Photo by Drs. A. A. M. van der Heyden, Naarden, the Netherlands

Few Dutch always dress in traditional clothing, but visitors can still see distinctive costumes, such as this one from the province of Overijssel.

Many towns in the Netherlands have water gates that allow canal traffic to pass beneath the city walls. The gate in Amersfoort dates from the fifteenth century, when the town was a prosperous hub of cloth production in the central Netherlands.

Photo by Drs. A. A. M. van der Heyden, Naarden, the Netherlands

Historically, the Dutch have worked hard to overcome economic challenges. They have successfully tackled tough goals, such as turning back the sea and providing generous benefits for all the nation's citizens. Dutch hard work will be needed in the 1990s, after EC member-nations form a closer economic union. The group has dismantled trade barriers and is promoting a common currency. These actions have made Europe a single trading bloc with more buying power. With a modern financial and communications network, the Netherlands is well positioned to prosper if its people and government can make the most of these new European opportunities.

Brokers scan their computer screens at the Amsterdam Stock Exchange. A major trading nation, the Netherlands has a fast, modern communications system and up-to-date financial institutions.

Courtesy of Netherlands Foreign Trade Agency (EVD)

63

Index